This
Nature Storybook
belongs to:

_____

_____

_____

WALKER BOOKS

For every blue whale alive today
there were once twenty.
People hunted and killed so many of them
that fewer than 10,000 remain.
Blue whales are now protected
and hunting them is banned,
so in some places their numbers are
growing — very, very slowly.
You could still sail the oceans for a year
and never see a single one.

For Joseph and Gabriel
N.D.

For Dilys
N.M.

First published 1997 by Walker Books Ltd
87 Vauxhall Walk, London SE11 5HJ

This edition published 2008

10 9 8 7 6 5 4 3 2 1

Text © 1997 Nicola Davies
Illustrations © 1997 Nick Maland

The right of Nicola Davies and Nick Maland
to be identified as author and illustrator respectively
of this work has been asserted by them in accordance
with the Copyright, Designs and Patents Act 1988

This book has been typeset in Monotype Centaur

Printed in China

British Library Cataloguing in Publication Data:
a catalogue record for this book
is available from the British Library

ISBN 978-1-4063-1257-7

www.walkerbooks.co.uk

BIG BLUE
WHALE

NICOLA DAVIES

illustrated by NICK MALAND

WALKER BOOKS
AND SUBSIDIARIES
LONDON · BOSTON · SYDNEY · AUCKLAND

The blue whale is big.

Bigger than a giraffe.

Bigger than an elephant.

Bigger than a dinosaur.

The blue whale is
the biggest creature
that has ever lived
on Earth!

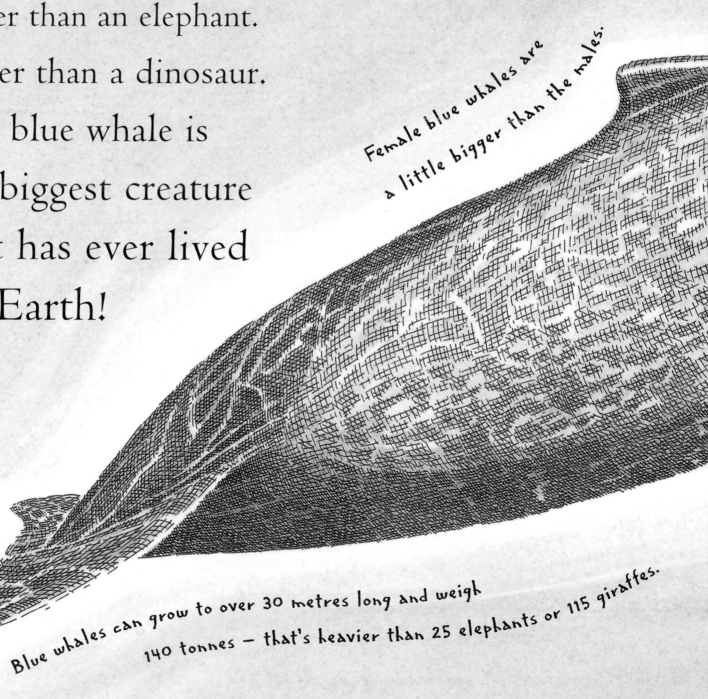

Female blue whales are
a little bigger than the males.

Blue whales can grow to over 30 metres long and weigh
140 tonnes – that's heavier than 25 elephants or 115 giraffes.

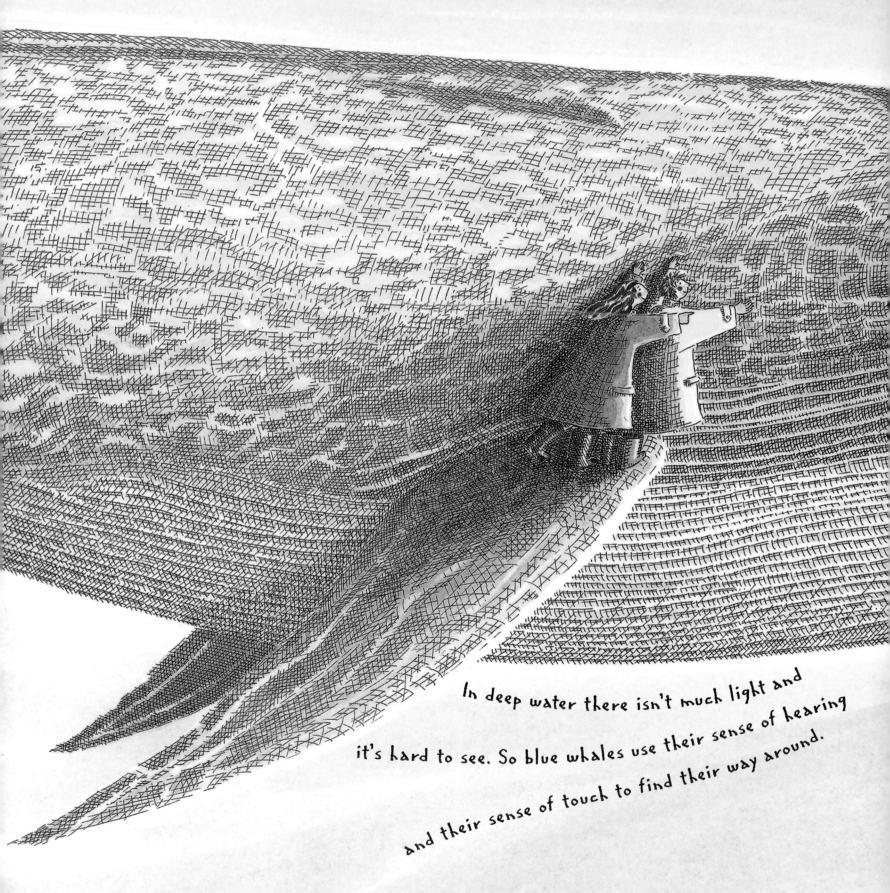

In deep water there isn't much light and it's hard to see. So blue whales use their sense of hearing and their sense of touch to find their way around.

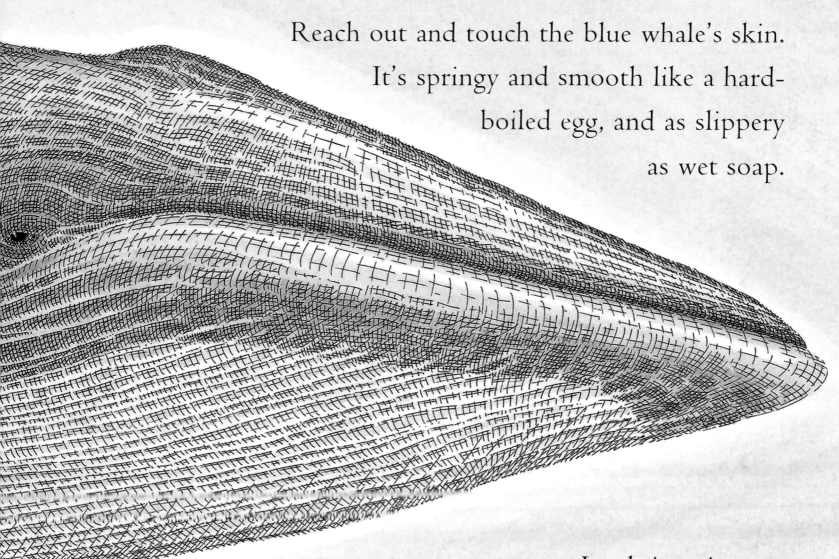

Reach out and touch the blue whale's skin.
It's springy and smooth like a hard-
boiled egg, and as slippery
as wet soap.

Look into its eye.
It's as big as a teacup and as dark
as the deep sea. Just behind the eye is a hole,
as small as the end of a pencil. The hole is one of
the blue whale's ears — sticking-out ears would
get in the way when the whale is swimming.

9

The blue whale lives all of its long life in the sea.
But it is a mammal like us, and it breathes air, not water.

From time to time, it has to come to the surface to breathe
through the blowholes on top of its head.

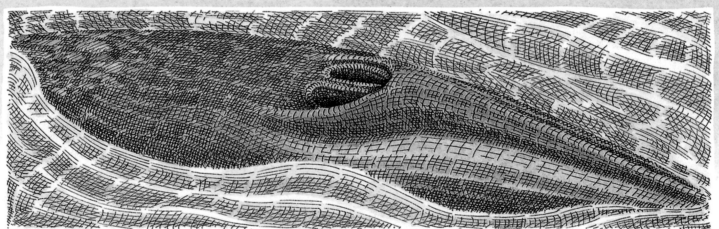

Blue whales can live for about 70 to 80 years.

When it breathes out,
it makes a great misty puff
as high as a house.
This is the whale's blow,
and you can see it from far away.
You can hear it, too – a great

PROOUFF.

And if you are close enough
you can smell it, as the whale's
breath is stale and fishy.

A blue whale can stay underwater for 30 minutes or more.
But on long journeys it usually surfaces for air every 2 to 5 minutes.

A blue whale can have
as many as 790 baleen plates in its mouth.
Baleen is tough bendy stuff, like extra-hard fingernails.

Take a look inside its mouth. Don't worry, the blue whale doesn't eat people. It doesn't even have any teeth. It has hundreds of baleen plates, instead. They're the long bristly things hanging down from its top jaw.

The whale doesn't need teeth for biting because its food is tiny!

The blue whale
eats krill – pale-pinkish,
shrimp-like creatures, the size
of your little finger.

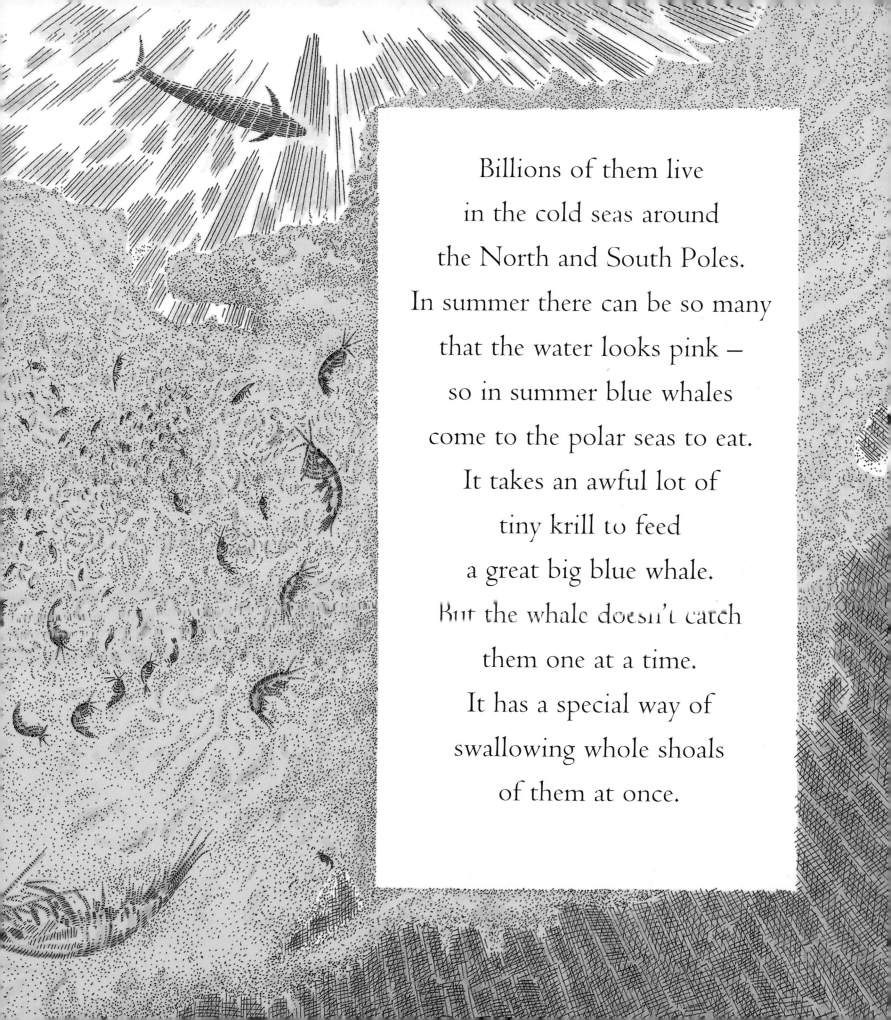

Billions of them live
in the cold seas around
the North and South Poles.
In summer there can be so many
that the water looks pink —
so in summer blue whales
come to the polar seas to eat.
It takes an awful lot of
tiny krill to feed
a great big blue whale.
But the whale doesn't catch
them one at a time.
It has a special way of
swallowing whole shoals
of them at once.

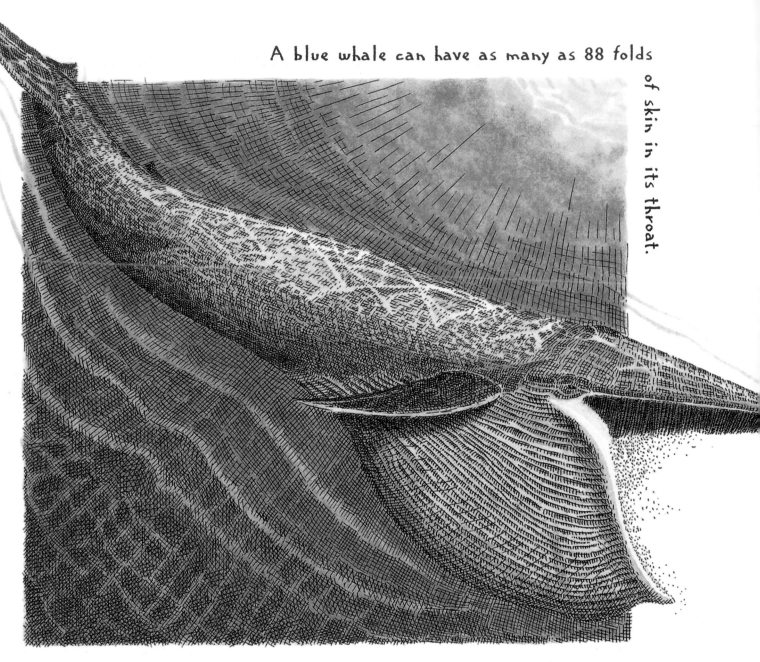

A blue whale can have as many as 88 folds of skin in its throat.

First, it takes a huge gulp of krill and salty seawater. There's room for all this because the whale's throat unfolds and opens out like a vast balloon. Then it uses its big tongue to push the water out between its bristly baleen plates.

The water streams away and leaves the krill caught
on the bristles like peas in a sieve.
Now all the whale has to do is lick them
off and swallow them.

A blue whale can eat about 30 million krill just in one
day – that's three big truck-loads!

And this is how the blue whale spends the summer — eating krill and getting fat. But in the autumn the polar seas freeze over.

In summer, the blue whale grows a thick layer of fat all over its body. This fat is called blubber, and it's a food store for the winter, when the whale eats very little.

18

The krill hide under the ice where the whale cannot catch them. So the whale swims away from the icy cold and the winter storms.

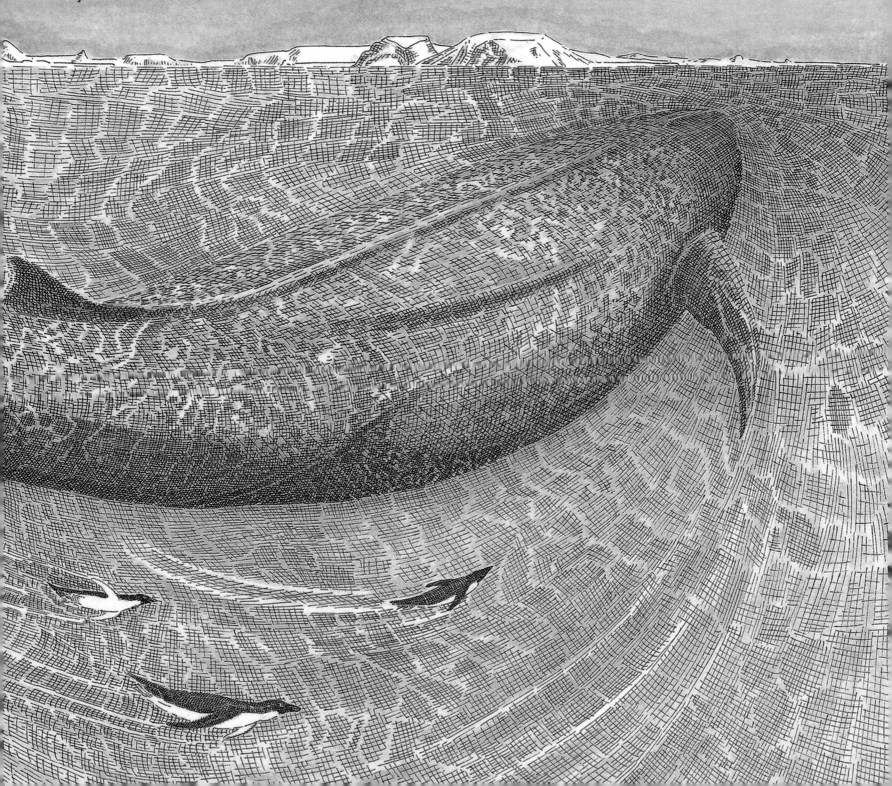

Day after day, the blue whale swims slowly and steadily towards its winter home. Its huge tail beats up and down to push it along. Its flippers steer it left or right.

For two months and more the whale swims, until at last it reaches the calm warm seas near the Equator.

There it stays all winter.

Some blue whales spend their summers around the South Pole and swim north to the Equator for the winter.

20

Others live around the North Pole and swim south for the winter.

North Pole

Atlantic
Ocean

Equator

Atlantic
Ocean

But when it's winter at the
South Pole, it's summer
at the North Pole.

So the two groups
of whales never meet.

And there the blue whale mother gives birth to her baby,
where storms and cold weather can't hurt it.

Male and female blue whales mate in winter and then part.
Babies are born about a year later.

The blue whale's baby slithers from her body, tail first.

Gently she nudges it to the surface to take its first breath.

Then the baby dives beneath her to take its first drink of milk.

A blue whale baby is 7 metres long at birth.
It drinks 600 litres of milk a day, sucking it from
the teats tucked into its mother's belly.

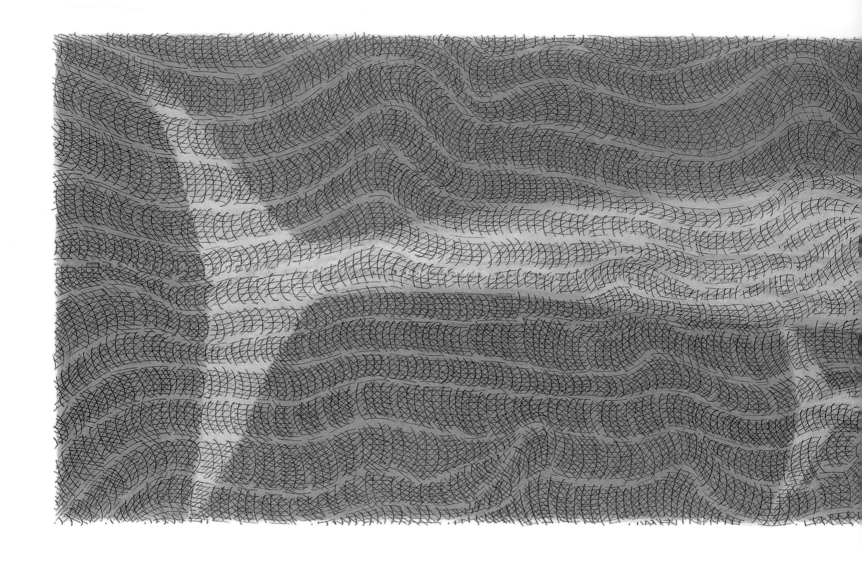

All through the winter, the blue whale keeps
her baby close. It feeds on her creamy milk,
and it grows and grows.
In spring, the two whales return to the polar seas
to feast on krill together. But by the autumn
the young whale is big enough to live on its own.

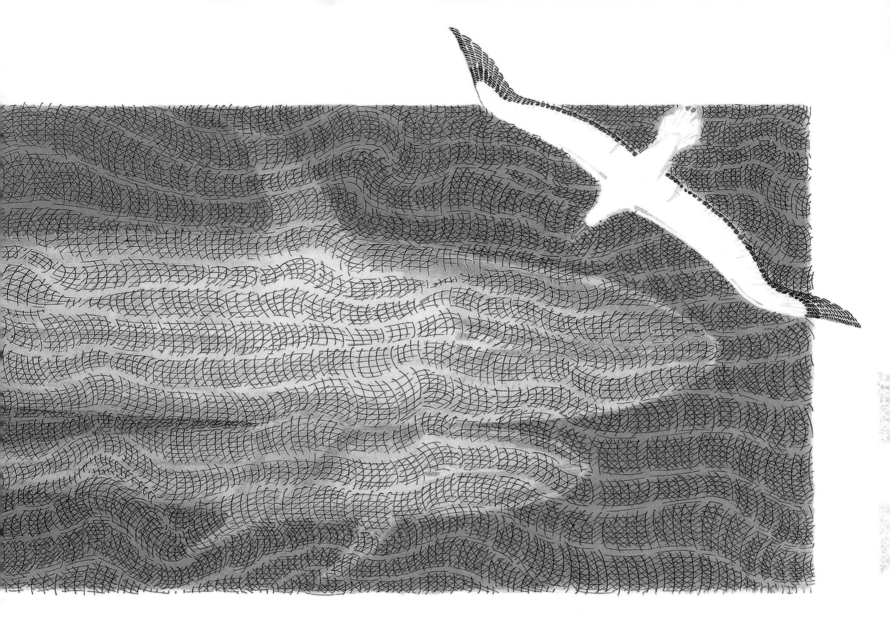

So mother and young whale part, and begin
the long journey back to the Equator.
A blue whale may travel from polar seas
to Equator and back every year of its life.
Sometimes it will swim with other blue whales,
but mostly it will swim alone.

Adult blue whales make their hums in deep water. It's much colder than near the surface, which helps the hum to travel a long way.

Yet, the blue whale may not be
as lonely as it seems.
Because sometimes it makes
a hum – a hum so loud and
so low that it can travel for
thousands of kilometres through
the seas, to reach other blue whales.
Only a very low hum could travel
so far. And only a very big animal
could make a hum so low.
Perhaps that's why blue whales
are the biggest creatures
on Earth – so that they can
talk to each other even when
they are far apart.
Who knows what they say.
"Here I am!" would be enough…

because in

the vastness

of the green seas,

even a blue whale is small

— and hard to find.

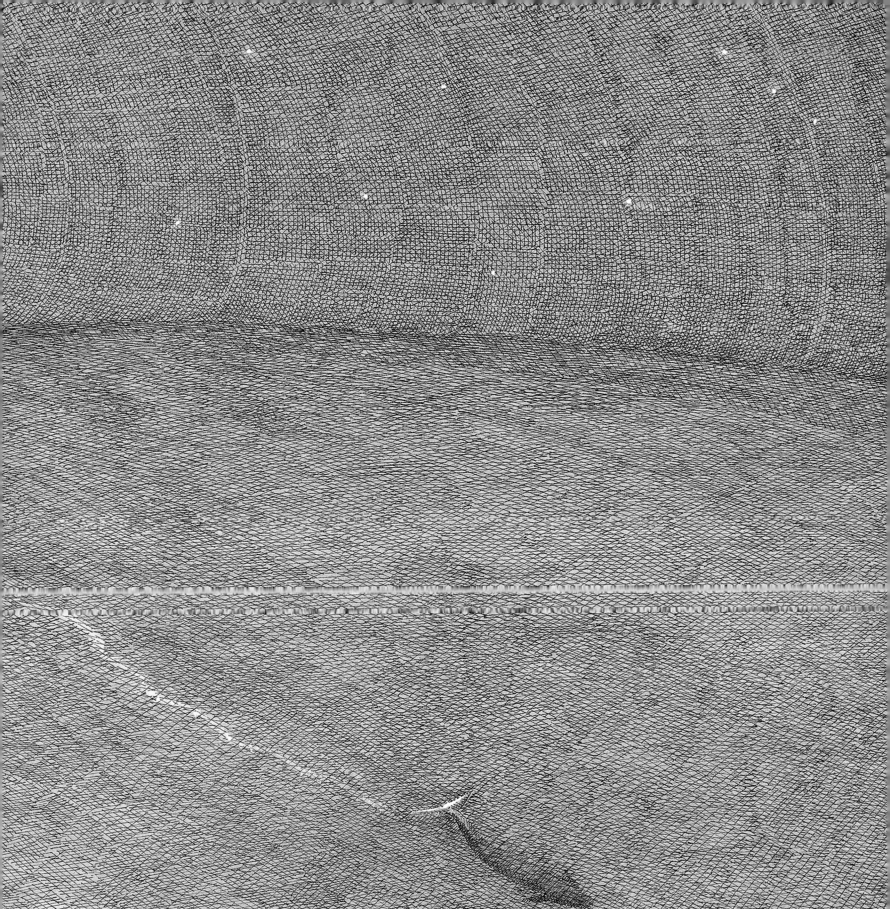

INDEX

Look up the pages to find out
about all these whale things.
Don't forget to look at both kinds
of word — this kind *and*
this kind.

About the Author

Nicola Davies is a zoologist who has studied all kinds
of mammals, from whales in the Indian Ocean and Newfoundland
to bats in west Wales. She is also the acclaimed author of many
books for children, including the Nature Storybooks *Ice Bear*,
One Tiny Turtle, *Bat Loves the Night* and *White Owl, Barn Owl*.
She lives in Devon.

About the Illustrator

Nick Maland worked as an actor before he took up drawing.
He has since illustrated many books for children, including *Glog*
by Pippa Goodhart and *Snip Snap* by Mara Bergman. In 2003
he was the overall winner of the V&A Illustration Awards.
He lives in London.

Praise for Nature Storybooks...

"For the child who constantly asks How? Why?
and What For? this series is excellent."
The Sunday Express

"A boon to parents seeking non-fiction picture books to read
with their children. They have excellent texts
and a very high standard of illustration to go with them."
The Daily Telegraph

"As books to engage and delight children, they work superbly.
I would certainly want a set in any primary
classroom I was working in."
Times Educational Supplement

"Here are books that stand out from the crowd,
each one real and individual in its own right and
the whole lot as different from most other series non-fiction
as tasty Lancashire is from processed Cheddar."
Books for Keeps

Find notes for teachers about how to use Nature Storybooks in the classroom at
www.walkerbooks.co.uk

Nature Storybooks support KS 1-2 Science